KArL MOORE

THE 18 RULES *of*
HAPPINESS

Simple, everyday attitudes for enjoying
profound happiness in your life

Inspire3 Publishing
20-22 Wenlock Road
London, N1 7GU

www.inspire3.com

Original Copyright © 2009 Karl Moore
Updated Version © 2016 Karl Moore

The author asserts the moral right to
be identified as the author of this work.

ISBN 978-1-4092-5866-7

Set in Minion and Bernhard Modern
Printed and bound in Great Britain

The 18 Rules of Happiness

Would YOU like to discover your own *true happiness?*

Right now, you spend 24 hours a day searching for happiness. It's the single motive behind absolutely every action you take.

But are you experiencing enough genuine happiness in your daily life?

If not, you need to take action.

This book is a mini-course in *mega-happiness*.

It unveils 18 simple secrets that you can use to begin enjoying *profound happiness* and freedom in your life.

From simple shifts in attitude to powerful mind-body "hacks this guide will show you how to easily tap into the *sunshine* that already exists within you - and, quite simply, become the *happiest person* you know.

What Others
Are Saying
About This Book

"Everyone should have a copy of this book on
their coffee table, in their bathroom, or on their
desk. It's a constant source of joy and inspiration,
never failing to make me smile each time I pick it
up and dip in."
- *Harvey Walsh, www.daytradingfreedom.com*

"In this book, Karl Moore shows all of us how we
can find happiness at any moment in our lives.
Unlike many self-development books, which often
take months to bring results, I found myself
smiling within the first few minutes. These 18
simple rules have the power to improve anyone's
life starting the minute they begin to read it. I
couldn't be happier."
– *John Derrick, www.johnderrick.com*

"Many people touch happiness just a few times in their lives. Some people, never at all. But in fact, it's possible to be happy all the time - if you know how. And who would have guessed? It's actually easy! Eons of wisdom are beautifully distilled here in this book, which demonstrates just how easy it is for you to be happy."

- Peter Shepherd, www.trans4mind.com

"Karl uses a simplistic style to pull back the curtain and expose what happiness is truly all about. Forget all the self-help hype - You will learn how easy it can be to accept, let go and move on to a happier, more fulfilling life. Great read Karl, thanks!"

- Gene Anger, www.best-self-help-sites.com

"Thanks to Karl Moore my income has grown 1,200% in two years. Karl has now come out with the secrets to his success. If you're looking for happiness in your life, I highly recommend this book. I've known Karl for years – and this is the only guide you'll ever need for finding true happiness in your life."

- Mark Anastasi, www.mark-anastasi.com

"This book is a reminder of what we should already know, but so often forget, about being happy. I love Rule #7, 'Be Happy Now.' Well, Karl - I am now that I've read your book and eventually remembered how!"

- Chris Lloyd, www.ultrabraintraining.com

"At last... Happiness made simple! Easy to understand and full of priceless wisdom, this book gave me a million 'Aha!' moments. You could almost open it to any page and get exalting inspiration you can use right now. This is the kind of book you always want to have handy when you need a boost. A real treasure. As for the author, I know him to be a man of integrity and a pure heart. I trust anything that comes from Karl."
– *Rebecca Marina, www.rebeccamarina.com*

"Pure wisdom! This book takes an ingenuous approach, with simple yet profound and deep insights! Karl undertakes to both entertain and educate in an unconventional means. You will love his humour. He has outlined simple steps to happiness - and he will take you there with no effort at all. My suggestion is to kick back and enjoy the ride with him!"
- *Evane Abbassi,*
www.alternatedisputeresolutioninc.com

"Was I ever 'happy' to discover this book! As an advocate of meditation, I deeply appreciated Karl's stance that in order to be truly happy, one must put themselves front and center - and peer right in. We must stop looking outside ourselves for measures of joy. This book beautifully illustrates how the light of peace and happiness are within each of us if we only let them shine. What an important tenet for our era!"
- *Daniel Topp, www.3pounduniverse.com*

"Karl gives his readers a road map to happiness! Besides sharing the 'how to do it' techniques and strategies to move steadily on the journey, he gives us inspiring quotes, a list of happy songs which you'll soon find yourself humming, and even feel good foods which will lift your mood and bring a smile to your face."
- *Sally K. O'Brien, www.sallykobrien.com*

"Nobody is more qualified to write these rules than Karl Moore. He is truly inspirational."
- *Carolyn Anderson, Kent Cancer Trust*

"We attract to our lives all our experiences and then we get to interpret them either in ways that support us or in ways that diminish the quality of our lives. So, what are the secrets to manifesting true and sustainable happiness in our lives? Karl Moore's latest book is a roadmap to making your life one filled with happiness and all the great things that are made possible by maintaining an attitude committed to finding endless opportunities for happiness. If you are ready to lead a happy and fulfilling life, this book is a great place to begin your journey."
- *Dr Joe Rubino, www.selfesteemsystem.com*

"In this book, Karl Moore has set out a road map anyone can follow to achieve a happier, more fulfilled lifestyle. I found this little book truly inspirational, and intend to put Karl's advice into practice every day from now on."
- *Nick Daws, www.mywritingblog.com*

"Many books have been written on the subject of happiness. Especially in the western world, where we have become happiness addicted. But if there's one book on happiness I would recommend, it's this one! Karl's book teaches the basic principles that happiness is always there, but needs to be cultivated to express itself. Very impressed with the clarity and profound insights this book delivers."
- *Thomas Herold, www.dreammanifesto.com*

"I absolutely love this book. I simply couldn't stop reading. If only I'd read something like this years ago! I never realised happiness was a choice, rather than a destination. Brilliant!"
– *Valerie Coburn, www.inspirationplus.net*

"Happiness is a choice. And it is indeed possible to be happy, when you choose to be so. These 18 rules are fundamental in changing the patterns that do not work for you – the ones that make you feel unhappy. When you follow these rules, you will indeed experience true happiness! In this book, Karl writes beautifully, his trademark style is both personable and likeable. It's hard not to be happy just by reading this book!"
- *Arabella Jolie, www.whyte-witch.com*

"This book is eye-opening in its simplicity – and a must-have for every household. Anyone that follows the 18 rules inside Karl's guide will inevitably enjoy an excellent lifetime journey."
– *J.Walker, www.natural-life-choices.com*

"Living joyfully is at the heart of life – which is why this book is an absolute must-read! Discover profound, lasting happiness and enjoy a more meaningful and fulfilling life simply by following Karl's timely and enlightened guidance. This guide will help you find your true joy in no time at all. Inspirational!"
- *Carol Anne Strange, www.carolannestrange.com*

"With much of the world popping Prozac, this book is one of those titles which should become compulsory reading! Light, easy to understand and written in that accessible, bright Karl Moore style, this book takes you by the hand and leads you into the garden of happiness, step-by-step. It will be on the recommended list of all my students — and quite frankly my friends and family as well. Happiness should be one of those things that's a given, and somehow it is elusive to so, so many. With Karl's help, you can open the door to happiness, just by opening any page, and reading his delectable wisdom."
- *Billie Dean, www.billiedean.com*

"Developing lasting happiness requires skill and time, plus a clear intention to change our attitude towards life. However, the actual thoughts, feelings and memories which have programmed us away from happiness may be difficult to identify. Karl Moore has provided us with a guide of 18 steps or rules to do just this, so that we may begin to fulfil our purpose for life with joy."
- *Johnathan Brooks, www.spiritbearcoaching.com*

"What a great book! A very succinct and easy to understand guide to happiness. I always knew that everyone could experience happiness in the moment – and Karl's book shows you how. Happiness come from within and this book shows you how to find it."
– *Will Thomas, www.tampabaydogwhisperer.com*

"When playing the game of life, people, events, and circumstances arrive almost magically to help us grow into our full potential and ultimately, bring happiness. After all, what are we doing here anyway if not to be happy? Everything we do is to that ultimate goal. Karl has given us a set of 'rules' for playing the game of life and shows us exactly how to win the happiness prize. Tap into the wisdom here - it will make you happy!"
- *Tom Murasso, www.borntomanifest.com*

"Fantastic! If you're looking for happiness in your life, this is the book for you. Read these simple 18 rules – and uncover a profound happiness and freedom denied to most. This book is a real breakthrough!"
– Larry Crane, www.releasetechnique.com

"I have known and have had the pleasure of working with Karl for about four years now within the self-development arena. I must tell you that if there are significantly more genuine and more inspiring individuals in this field today I haven't met them... and let me tell you I've met just about everybody. It's no accident that he was hand selected as one of the 12 key teachers in The Meta Secret movie and the reasoning for which is 100% clear within only a few seconds of reading this book. Karl is a true visionary and I'm very thankful to call him a friend."
- Joe DePalma, www.readysetrise.com

About the Author

Karl Moore is an entrepreneur and self-development leader.

He has spent over 15 years exploring the world of personal improvement, and is a featured teacher from the movie *Think*.

Karl is the author of six best-selling books, including *The 18 Rules of Happiness*.

You can visit Karl's official website at www.karlmoore.com.

"Some pursue happiness, others create it."

- Unknown

Contents

Foreword
by David Riklan

We're all looking for happiness.

It's the hidden meaning behind absolutely everything we do. It's what drives us to work, to explore relationships, to improve our health, to read books like this.

Yet how many of us truly find happiness in our lives?

As founder of the Web's most popular online self improvement site, I can authoritatively state – not too many!

This book is a reminder of what happiness truly is, and how you can recognize it in your life. You see, every single one of us stumbles across happiness on a daily basis.

But most of us simply stand up again, brush ourselves down, and stride on. They fail to recognize the opportunity they just missed!

This book will reawaken you to the happiness in your life.

Karl Moore has been my friend for many years now. We recently appeared in The Meta Secret movie together, and he's known for his perpetually optimistic outlook.

Not only that, he's also one of the most successful businessmen you'll ever meet – not that this humble man will ever openly admit to the fact.

This man knows about success, about freedom, about spirituality – but most of all, about happiness.

So, sit back and let the Karl share his happiness secrets for experiencing even more joy in your life.

I guarantee the journey will amaze you.

David Riklan
Founder, www.selfgrowth.com

Introduction

Every single one of us spends 24 hours a day in search of happiness.

Everything we do, every action we take, is intended to take us closer to happiness, and away from pain. Think about it. Our lives are dedicated to the quest of being happy.

In fact, it's so important that those very words are honoured in the USA constitution, which enshrines the right to "life, liberty, and the pursuit of happiness."

But when was the last time you took a course on happiness?

Did they teach you how to be happy at school or college? Have you ever attended a seminar on the topic? In fact, when was the last time you even consciously THOUGHT about your own happiness?

This book is YOUR guide to happiness.

It provides 18 simple "rules" designed to help you discover the happiness that exists inside your own world – right now.

Every day, most of us focus on the grey clouds in the sky. Life is dim and gloomy, and showers are just minutes away. But we forget something.

We don't remember that just behind those clouds, the sun is beaming brightly – every single minute of every single day.

This book has just one purpose. To help you blow away your own grey clouds – and bask in your own beautifully happy sun.

Inside these pages, you'll find 18 simple rules designed to shift your perspective, helping you to rediscover the happiness you may have forgotten.

The rules range from simple shifts in perspective – such as the realization that small things don't really matter, which often comes after a close family member dies – through to actual techniques we can use to become happier - such as learning how to release, saying yes more, or increasing our Omega 3 intake.

They're simple. They're elegant. They're easy.

And they're in your hands – right now.

So, let this be your guide toward happiness.

Treasure these rules, embrace them in your everyday life – and smile!

Karl Moore
www.karlmoore.com

How to Use
This Book

Using this book is easy. Because happiness is simple!

You can read through this book in traditional fashion, from start to finish. The more you read it, the more you'll find the principles within becoming part of your everyday life.

Try to read the book a couple of times in the first week, then at least once a month thereafter.

If you can, keep a copy in your restroom and read a randomly-selected rule every time you visit. Or store a copy by your bed for a little morning or night-time inspiration.

You could also give copies to friends and family, to help inject a little extra happiness into their lives – and just to show them you care.

Be sure to give attention to the appendices in this book too, particularly appendix #1, "A Short Course in Releasing." The techniques taught in this section are referred to throughout the book, and are incredibly helpful in uncovering your own inner harmony.

You may also wish to read "The Secret Art of Self-Development" (Karl Moore, ISBN 978-0-9559935-0-3), which serves as the perfect spiritual accompaniment to this book.

So, ready to dive into your own true happiness?

Read on.

Rule #1 - Stop Feeling Sorry for Yourself!

*"Self-pity is our worst enemy
and if we yield to it, we can
never do anything wise in
this world." - Helen Keller*

Oh, come on. Admit it.

We all do it every single day.

Everybody enjoys wallowing in a little self-pity.
It feels great to remind ourselves how terrible the
world is. How we've not been given the right
opportunities. How people are against us. How
life has been a real struggle this past year.

Right?

But here's a true secret to happiness. And it's probably the biggest, easiest and quickest happiness secret you'll stumble across. Ever.

If you want to be happy – just stop feeling sorry for yourself.

Self-pity, you see, is the worst kind of emotion. It eats up everything around, except itself. Soon, self-pity is all that exists, and you're left feeling sorry for how poorly life has been treating you.

We've all felt like that, right?

Maybe you feel like life has dealt you a bad hand. Perhaps you've lost money, family or health. It could be that you've missed out on so many opportunities that others have been easily granted – and you think that fate really HAS been unfair to you.

And that viewpoint might even be 100% correct.

But STOP feeling sorry for yourself.

It's not going to help the situation. It'll only help you to wallow in a state of apathy, playing the victim. The kind of person that things happen to, but that can't do anything about it. By stopping feeling sorry for yourself, you can actually get on and DO something about it.

Trust me on this one. This is the biggest ever technique for putting a smile onto your face.

If you want to be happy – stop feeling sorry for yourself.

You could close this book right now and you'd already hold the wisdom of ten thousand self-development courses, and double that number of self-help gurus.

And it's so simple. In fact, it's worth repeating (and rewording) one more time:

Stop feeling sorry for yourself – and you will be happy.

Rule #2 –
Be Grateful

*"If the only prayer you ever say
in your entire life is thank
you, it will be enough."*
- Meister Eckhardt

We live in a fast-paced, microwave, drive-thru,
Buy-It-Now society.

It's a society that has forgotten to be truly grateful
for the things around it. We only tend to be
grateful for things when we no longer have them.

Think of the sense of relief you gain when you just
get over an illness, and are so thankful that your
turbulent tummy has now settled. Consider how
appreciative you are when those tests come back
clear. Or when the speeding camera doesn't flash.
Or when you finally find your lost child in the
supermarket.

These are the moments in life when we realise how blessed we truly are.

Yet how many of us truly appreciate that on a day-to-day basis?

My guess is very few of us. We only become grateful of things when we think we don't have them.

But here's the thing: by counting our blessings every day, in a very literal way, we become happier people. Research across the globe in countless studies has proven this over and over again.

So, when was the last time YOU were truly grateful?

Think of all the wonderful things you have to be grateful for right now. It could be your family. Or your health. Maybe your home. Your friends. Your brain. Your heart. Your spirit. Even your DVD collection.

We've all got amazing things in our own lives that make us smile with joy. Things that bring a secret, loving tear to our eyes.

And if we can only learn to count these blessings every day, we'll discover a true happiness and greater appreciation of the beautiful world we surround ourselves with.

So, if you can, make that part of your daily ritual. Count your blessings, briefly in the morning, and briefly at night. Then smile at the world for sending such great things your way.

Be grateful – and you will be happy.

Rule #3 – Say Yes More

*"I will say yes to every favour,
request, suggestion and
invitation. I will swear to say
yes where once I would say no."*
– Danny Wallace

"No!" is a wonderful word.

It's powerful, it's universally understood, and it stops everything in its tracks. By saying no, you're instantly slamming the door and holding it shut, ensuring nothing else gets through.

But how many of us say "No!" way too often?

You see, "No" really holds us back in life. It closes us off to many of life's wonderful experiences, and causes us to resist what happens around us.

When we say no, we're swimming against the current. When we say yes, we're swimming with the current.

Which do you think is easiest? Which produces less stress? Which is faster, and more enjoyable?

We say "NO!" to life's funny randomness, when a passing bus splashes rainwater all over our new jeans. We shout "NO!" to our emotions, resisting and fighting grief, when our pet rat passes away. We yell "NO!" when we don't get that promotion, which we'd been working so hard to achieve.

Long story short: we say NO to everything, too often.

We fight against what happens to us in life, rather than allowing it to be as it is. We resist it, rather than accepting it. We say "No!" rather than saying "Yes" – or even just "Okay."

By saying "Yes!" more to life, we go with the flow. Things become more enjoyable and positive, less stressful and anxious, and often the situation turns out for the better regardless.

So, SAY YES MORE.

And what about saying "Yes!" more socially too? Say "Yes!" when you're invited to that party. Say "Yes!" when you're asked if you'd like lunch with the boys. Say "Yes!" when you've asked to go on that speed dating night, which you wouldn't normally even consider.

(That's what Danny Wallace did in his great comedy cum self-help book, *Yes Man*. He said yes more. It changed his life.)

So, if you'd like to flow more with the current of life... If you'd like to inject a little more excitement into your day... If you'd like to enjoy the random twist and turns of fate...

Then SAY YES MORE.

The Australians call it a "bias for yes." The Spanish say "Si a todo." Buddhists describe it as flowing with the river of life. In this book, we simply *say yes more*.

Try it out, even if just for a week. It'll change your world.

Say yes more – and you will be happy.

Rule #4 – Follow Your Bliss

"When you follow your bliss, doors will open where you would not have thought there would be doors; and where there wouldn't be a door for anyone else." – Joseph Campbell

In life, it's easy to end up in the "wrong place."

We're doing a job we hate. We're living with people we dislike. We're keeping secrets, when we'd rather be open and genuine.

We get stuck and don't feel authentic, because we're not truly doing what we want.

Does that sound like you?

If so, you need to find what makes you truly happy.

American mythologist Joseph Campbell summed up that process of seeking your own true happiness and authenticity in three simple words: "Follow your bliss."

Sometimes in life, we all stray and lose direction. We're half-way up a ladder we didn't want to climb, rather than at the bottom of one that we do. By not following our bliss, we permanently limit our happiness and stop ourselves truly enjoying our lives.

Are you following *your* bliss?

One thing bliss is not – and that's money.

Bliss is what you're doing when you're wrapped up in the moment. When you're so thrilled just to be doing it, it ceases even to be work anymore. Your bliss occurs when you're living in the moment, and time doesn't really matter anymore.

My bliss is helping to run a number of really big businesses, while teaching self-development. In fact, I love it so much that I'm typing this rule while on holiday in Thailand. It's not for the money, it's for the pleasure. I'm immersed in my own bliss.

So, what's YOUR bliss?

You may love teaching tube surfing on the beaches of Australia. Or running your own small accountancy firm. Or helping teenagers discover and appreciate the world of art.

When you were a child, and played with a kite, you were immersed in your bliss.

As an adult, what makes you feel like that again? And how can you increase that in your life?

Follow your bliss.

You know, I have a theory that absolutely everyone in life knows what they need to do in order to become happy. It's just that most aren't brave enough to take the steps to do it.

So, that's your challenge.

Take those steps, follow your bliss – and you will be happy.

Rule #5 – Learn to Let Go

"By letting it go it all gets done.
The world is won by those who
let it go. But when you try and
try, the world is beyond the
winning." – Lao Tzu

Emotions are the things that make us human.

When we cry, we're experiencing emotion. When we're fearful, we're experiencing emotion. Whenever we're angry, upset, passionate, greedy, scared – we're experiencing emotion.

But sometimes emotions need reining in!

They cause us not to make that fantastic speech at the company conference, because we're *scared* of the platform. They stop us making up with long-gone friends, because we're still *maddened* with anger. They cause us to stay in relationships that damage us, because we're still *emotionally addicted* to the misshapen void the relationship fills.

Emotions aren't always good for you. You are NOT your emotions.

Emotions are just things that happen, and which you can (and should) control.

Sure, that *sounds* easy. But here's the thing: it actually really *is* easy.

The best way to let go of our troublesome emotions, the emotions that are holding us back from happiness, is to discover the art of *releasing*.

So, what is releasing?

Releasing is the ability to realize that you are desperately "gripping" onto emotions in your life. You treat them as if they're "you." It's about realising you can let go of them, unclench your fist around them, just by making a simple decision.

How can you start releasing?

The simplest method is just to go through your life, recognizing where emotions are holding you up. Are you angry about your home-life situation? Your working hours? That incident you just had, with the rude guy at the grocery store?

Bring that issue or situation to the forefront of your mind. Connect with the emotion.

Then, ask yourself: "Can I let this go?"

Can you let it go? Just for this moment? Could you release this emotion?

Breathe out, and answer honestly with either "Yes" or "No." Either answer is absolutely fine.

If you can let it go, then do it. Really *feel* yourself letting go. *Feel* yourself releasing, unclenching, relaxing, detaching. It should feel something like when a doctor calls to tell you those worrying tests have come back all clear: an immediate release of worry and tension.

And if you can't let go right now, don't stress it. Give yourself permission to hold onto it some more. It's your decision.

How does that feel? If the emotion still has charge, simply repeat the process until you feel better – or until you feel like stopping.

Remember, letting go doesn't mean you "forgive" the person at the grocery store, or you "allow" that kind of behaviour. It just means that you release the negative emotion inside of *you*.

By releasing negative emotions, you'll not only enjoy much more freedom in your life – you'll also become more emotionally stable and less stressed too.

So, learn to let go – and you will be happy.

(PS. Releasing is so important, I've included a how-to mini-course at the end of this book. It's in Appendix I: "A Short Course in Releasing.")

Rule #6 – Do Random Acts of Kindness

"If you want others to be happy, practice compassion. If you want to be happy, practice compassion." - Dalai Lama

We've all felt it.

That spark of happiness which ignites within us whenever we do a good deed for someone else.

We hold open the door for the elderly lady behind us, and she returns the favour with a loving, grandmother's smile. You bring a box of chocolates into work for no particular reason, and get the warm attention of all your colleagues.

The truth is that doing things for other people really makes US feel great!

The more we give, the more we receive.

And one perfect way to add a little extra happiness to your own life, and the outside world, is to indulge in *Random Acts of Kindness*. Or RAKs as I prefer to abbreviate.

So, what are Random Acts of Kindness?

Well, the clue is really in the name. A RAK is a small act of kindness that you grant to someone else in the world – for absolutely no reason whatsoever, without expecting anything in return.

The classic example of a RAK is to pay at a toll booth for the car behind you. The recipient of the Random Act of Kindness will not only be flattered and uplifted by your generous deed, it's likely they'll "pay it forward" to someone else too. And that person may pay it forward yet again.

Indeed, your single Random Act of Kindness *could* just change the world.

So, what Random Acts of Kindness could YOU indulge in – to make yourself, and the world around you, happier?

Donate to a charity shop. Give someone a hug. Write a letter of appreciation. Say "I love you" to your parents. Pay for someone behind you. Donate blood. Scrape the ice off a stranger's car windscreen.

Do something for them that they can't.

Give $1 of your money in the best way you can. Become a conservation volunteer. Give your groceries to a neighbour. Take someone out for the day. Spend time with a local elder. Send someone a bunch of flowers, randomly.

Take chocolate into work for sharing, without a reason. Thank your mentor for their support. Plant a tree. Pick up litter. Be someone's biggest fan for a day. Be nice to someone who looks low. Smile more. Give food to a nearby shelter. Hold open the door. Give a cup of food at www.thehungersite.com.

Remember, it doesn't have to be exuberant, and it doesn't have to cost you a penny.

Just throw a little extra kindness out to the world – and watch how you find greater happiness starting to flood back into your own life.

So, do Random Acts of Kindness – and you will be happy.

Rule #7 –
Happiness Is
Only Ever Now

"Few of us ever live in the present, we are forever anticipating what is to come or remembering what has gone." - Louis L'Armor

Some years ago, it was traditional in many British pubs to have an infamous sign hanging above the bar:

"Free Beer Tomorrow!"

It's funny because, of course, "tomorrow" never comes.

But when you think about it, how many of us truly live our lives like that?

We spend so much time waiting to be happy in the future, or worrying about the past, that we forget to live in the moment. We fail to realise that happiness can only EVER be *now*.

Let me give you an example. You're driving through the city and your favourite song hits the radio. You're stuck in traffic, but loving the music – and you start to crazily sing along. You really get into it. You're in the moment. But then you catch a few jealous faces in nearby cars, and go all shy and timid.

Suddenly you're no longer living in the moment. You're wondering what they'll think about you. You're concerned they'll disapprove. You freeze up. Your happiness has gone, and your inhibition has arrived. You're no longer in the moment, in the NOW – you're stuck thinking about wanting approval from these people, worried what they'll think of you outside that moment.

Right?

Try to catch yourself at some random point today – and just check what's on your mind. If you're like most people, you'll be somewhere other than *here* and *now*.

You'll be thinking about whether you made a good impression with that guy earlier today. You might be thinking about the holiday you have planned for next September. Or how all of your problems will be solved this time next year.

You'll be *anywhere* but in the MOMENT. In fact, we each spend 95% of our time in the *past* or the *future*.

But here's the thing: Life is transient. The past has gone. The future is just a dream. The only time that truly exists *ever* is RIGHT NOW.

In other words, RIGHT NOW is the ONLY time you can do or change ANYTHING in your life.

You are only ever what exists in THIS MOMENT.

So, are you HAPPY right now? Are you doing EVERYTHING you'd like to – and feeling THRILLED with life, as you read these words? If you're not, then make the decision to be happy. NOW.

And if you'd like, put down this book, and go fly a kite. Or tell your partner that you love them. Or get your groovy flares on and head out to the nearby disco.

NOW is the only time you can change anything. And NOW is the only time you have.

So, make that simple decision – to be happy NOW.

Rule #8 –
Experience,
Don't Hoard!

"When you're curious, you find lots of interesting things to do." – Walt Disney

We all dream of fast cars, expensive yachts and magnificent showcase homes.

But do these things really make us happy?

Research says – well, *yes*, actually. Let's be honest. Anyone that says they're happy while stone broke is probably lying. Having a little money behind you is always a great idea. Money makes things happen.

But even so, studies have shown that the happiness "created" by material goods is only ever temporary.

Within a few months, the dog hairs have permanently settled into the back seat of your once-new Mercedes – and annoying neighbours have moved next door to your beach home in Santa Monica.

The initial rush these material pleasures once brought soon subsides.

So, how do you get a lasting buzz from your money?

Well, those same studies showed that investing in *experiences* rather than *material goods* created greater lasting happiness.

From travelling in the tropics to overnight on the Orient Express, mini "life adventures" brought with them an immediate thrill – and a lasting memory and experience of the world, which resulted in greater long-term happiness.

So, rather than hoarding your cash, or spending it on merely material pleasures – why not indulge in a few mini life adventures of your own?

Go on a safari holiday in Africa. Visit the location of your favourite film. Hunt down the Aurora Borealis at the tip of Sweden. Take two weeks out and explore your own country.

Learn a new language. Visit your local tourist board and follow their recommendations. Get involved in a nearby wine tasting group. Discover ballroom dancing.

It doesn't have to be big and it doesn't have to be expensive. And you can always do it on your own, too.

Even more exciting, set yourself crazy challenges and see what happens. Write a blog, or book, about your experiences.

Say "Yes!" to everything for a week and see what happens. Date twenty men over two months. Dine out somewhere new every night for two weeks. Meet five new people every day for a week. Go out with a new group of friends every week for two months. Find five people on the Internet with the same name as you – and try to meet one of them.

By living, and truly *experiencing* life, we feel more whole, fulfilled and authentic.

So, experience – don't hoard – and you will be happy.

Rule #9 –
Appreciate
Both Sides
of the Coin

*"You don't know when you've
hit a peak until you're coming
down. And you don't know
when you've hit a trough until
you're climbing out. It's all good"
– David Brent*

The world is crammed full of "opposites."

In order to have *hot*, you must have *cold*. In order
to have *light*, you must also have *dark*. In order to
have *up*, you must have *down*.

Right? They're opposites. One can't really exist without the other.

In fact, they're actually "pairs." Without each other, neither can exist. It just doesn't make sense. You can't have *up* without *down*.

We all understand that now.

But how many times do we try to cram our lives with *happiness* – and remove every last drop of *sadness*?

The truth is that in order for you to experience true happiness in your life, you *must* experience sadness. It's required. Without sadness, we really can't even understand what happiness is.

Yet how many of us struggle and fight against sadness when it comes into our lives?

We think that we should ONLY be experiencing the good, the positive, the happy. We MUST be thinking positively at all times. And if we don't, we blame ourselves for failing.

Is this a realistic way to live your life? Are YOU addicted to only experiencing the "good" in life?

Are you TRULY embracing the "duality" of your life experiences?

Remember, you cannot throw only the heads side of a coin. The tails side always goes with it. In order to have happiness, you must also experience sadness. If you wish, consider it a "credit" toward future happiness.

Dolly Parton describes it much more eloquently: "If you want the rainbow, you've got to put up with the rain."

In other words, and quite simply: It's all good.

Stop judging individual experiences, and how "good" or "bad" they are. Just enjoy and embrace all your life adventures. And when seemingly negative things happen, remember that it's just the duality of life. It's just the other side of the coin. It's *required*. It's part of the equation.

So, appreciate the other side of the coin – and you will be happy.

Rule #10 – Be More Social

"Let us be grateful to people who make us happy, they are the charming gardeners who make our souls blossom."
- Marcel Proust

It turns out that Michael Caine was right all along.

Playing Scrooge in the *Muppets Christmas Carol*, he sang: "If you want to know the measure of a man, you simply count his friends!"

Countless studies on the science of happiness have turned up one single characteristic of the happiest and most successful people in society.

They have a large social network!

Lots of friends. Lots of colleagues. Lots of people they call just to banter with for 10 minutes.

How many friends are stored in *your* cell phone?

One shortcut to becoming happier – quickly – is to simply make more friends.

Be proactive about it. Don't just wait for interesting people to stumble into your life. Join a local dance group. Discover a book club. Try randomly chatting with strangers in your nearest cafe.

Get yourself listed on social networking sites, such as Facebook, Google+, MySpace, Bebo, Hi5 – and join the online groups that share your interests. Subscribe to the many friendship-only sites springing up in big cities. Get *out* there!

Making friends isn't that difficult. You just need to make the effort.

Here are some tips.

Firstly, make yourself an *attractive* friend. Don't begrudge buying a coffee occasionally. Don't have "attitude." Don't spend your time moaning. Nobody likes negativity. Keep a smile on your face – while being yourself.

Secondly, make an effort, even when they don't. Sometimes people are reserved in the early stages of friendship, and need that extra push before a real connection can be established. Be the one to make that move. If it doesn't work out, it's their loss. Move on.

Throughout it all, however, make sure you play the numbers game.

Don't stop when you have one or two extra friends. Keep going and going. Expand your social circle as far as you can. Be the person that walks through town and bumps into a dozen friends.

Remember, the happiest people are those that have the largest social circles.

So, be more social – and you will be happy.

Rule #11 –
Love More!

"Love and kindness are never
wasted. They always make a
difference. They bless the
one who receives them, and
they bless you, the giver."
– Barbara De Angelis

American spiritual master Lester Levenson was
given just days to live.

The doctors had little hope for his failing heart.
But, surviving a few days longer than expected,
Lester turned to consider what life was all really
about. (He zoomed out. Rule #17.)

He concluded that life was about happiness,
freedom. These were the things he needed to
pursue.

But what granted him the most freedom and happiness in life?

Lester instantly felt that the answer was *love*. And when his many girlfriends expressed their love for him in public, certainly he felt a wave of happiness.

Yet it was fleeting. Momentary.

Then he realised that he felt the *most* happy in life – when *he* was the one giving the love!

The more he loved his girlfriend, the happier he became. The more he loved the world around him, the happier he became. The more he loved even his enemies, the happier he became.

And best of all, HE could control the amount of love he gave – and thereby control the amount of happiness he experienced.

Think about it for a moment. Doesn't that ring true for you?

Don't you feel happier when you are *loving more?*

I'm not talking about the clingy, relationship love that most people are well-aware of. But rather an open, giving, warm love. An all-accepting love, like that of a mother for her child, or a child for his puppy.

So, can you simply begin to *love more?*

For absolutely no reason at all. Just for fun. Love the whole world more.

Love your family for being as maddening as they are. Love the beautiful green trees around you as you take your daily stroll. Love your friends for all of their strengths and weaknesses. Love both sides of the coin. (Rule #10.) Simply, *love more*.

Even your enemies, or that rude guy that insulted you this very morning. Remember, if you'd travelled in their footsteps and had their experiences in life right to that very moment, whatever they just did would make perfect sense to you. Accept it, and give them a little love, because they might just need it.

Go through everyone you know – and in your own mind, offer them a little love. Keep that open heart as you walk around during your day.

Because, as the Beatles suggested, love might just be all you need.

So, love more – and you will be happy.

Rule #12 –
Have a Dream

"A person starts dying when they stop dreaming."
– Brian Williams

Learning how to be happy NOW is a real skill.
(Rule #7.)

They say he who is not happy with what he has,
will not be happy with what he gets.

But it's equally as important to have a dream to
lead you forward in life.

Everyone who ever did *anything* started with a
dream, a vision, a goal, a thought. Coupled with
that distinctly human quality, *hope.*

So, what do YOU dream of?

Would you like to explore the ancient castles of
England? Would you like to act in a local theatre

production? Would you like to write your first novel? Or even your second?

Perhaps you dream of helping your son through college. Or owning a second home in Miami. Or starting your own online business. Or having the very best family Christmas ever.

Or ... ?

Dreams are critical. They light up life.

Without them, we become bored, and tired, and apathetic.

So, take this opportunity to really clarify your dreams. Take a pen and paper and spend an hour figuring out what you really dream about.

Create a scrapbook and fill it with magazine pictures. Write your dreams on special paper, and put them in an envelope under your pillow. Scribble them onto scrap paper and burn it at midnight with a yellow candle, if you wish.

It doesn't really matter how you record them, ritual or no ritual. But clarify your dreams, and write them down. They'll suddenly take on a new importance, and you'll automatically find yourself heading closer toward them. (See Rule #13.)

But whatever you do, make sure you have a dream. They're incredibly important.

Dreams are the spark plugs of the spirit.

Make sure yours are ready for action.

So, have a dream – and you will be happy.

Rule #13 –
Intention Sets
Direction

*"Whether you think you can or you can't,
you're right." – Henry Ford*

Have you ever set out for a party, expecting it to
be *terrible* – and it was?

Ever left for a party, expecting it to be *brilliant* –
and it was?

You might not have realised this in your life yet,
however the outcome you *expect* is often the
outcome you *get*.

You wake up on a bright, sunny day, yawn and
stretch your way out of a comfortable bed, and

decide that you have a wonderful 16 waking hours ahead of you. And you have a great day!

The next morning, you wake to grey clouds and heavy rain, stub your toe on the bed, and decide that today is a bad day. And guess what? Strangely, you're right again.

Here's a simple way of putting this that you may not have thought of before:

Your intention sets your direction.

In other words, the route you plan out for yourself is most likely the one you'll end up taking.

If you expect something great to happen, it often does. If you expect that things will go wrong, they probably will too.

Of course, the actual event itself likely won't change. However if you anticipate a great party, you'll automatically filter out the negatives and set yourself in a mood to enjoy to the max. If you're in doom and gloom mode, you'll focus on one tiny argument in the background somewhere, and let it spoil your whole evening. It's entirely relative.

Because your intention sets your direction.

This is really the principle on which the whole self-development community is current thriving. The Law of Attraction, *The Secret*, *What The Bleep*, Cosmic Ordering – even prayer. They're all describing a convoluted form of this incredibly simple principle.

They hype it up. They give it weird names. They surround it with mystical ritual. But the core concept remains the same.

Decide on where you're going and how it'll be for you – and it'll happen.

There's a great line in *Alice in Wonderland*, where the Cheshire Cat advises: "If you don't know where you're going, any road will take you there."

So, the next time you go anywhere, or do anything, set your intention first. Make it clear that you're going to have a great time, you'll meet some fantastic people, and that it's going to be wonderful.

Set your general intention every morning and every night, too. The brighter and more positive, the better. Remember to set intention with your dreams, as well. (Rule #12.)

It's simple.

Set your sunny intention – and you will be happy.

Rule #14 – Enjoy Simple Pleasures

"Simplicity is the essence of happiness."
- Cedric Bledsoe

Too often, our lives are filled with complex demands and desires.

We get upset because our new Sony Vaio has a deep red fascia rather than the grey-black we preferred. We're annoyed because our restroom underfloor heating isn't quite as warm as we'd like – and, come to think of it, those bathroom tiles are a little out-of-date.

How often do you find yourself criticising what exists in your life – rather than appreciating it?

And how often do you take time out to truly enjoy the really SIMPLE pleasures in life?

Enjoying simple pleasures is, truly, one of the real secrets to happiness.

It's an attitude. The ability to appreciate the happiness, the beauty, the pleasure in the simple things around us.

The gloriously rich taste of a British Sunday roast. The cool sensation of a spring breeze. That familiar, homely smell of your dog. Sitting around with your family, laughing at some television comedy.

Not only that, happiness can also be found in simple routines, too.

That daily "thinking space" walk around a nearby river. That warm early morning cup of coffee before the working day begins. The weekly game of chess you play with an elderly neighbour. That sneaky glass of wine while unwinding with your husband.

These are the simple pleasures and routines that bring us happiness.

Happiness does not have to be complex.

For me, happiness can be found on a cold Friday night, wrapped up in my quilt, a re-run of Columbo playing on television, and a warm mug of tea in my hand. To me, that's true bliss. It gives me a warm, cosy feeling even as I write this.

So, what simple pleasures and rituals currently exist in your life?

And if you don't have any, take time out to generate a few for yourself.

Soak up the sunset tomorrow evening. Go to church every week, if only for the atmosphere. Cook yourself an experimental, flavour-filled meal. Indulge your senses. Drive to the sea.

Remember the simple things that you truly enjoy. Then take time out to experience them again. Or even better, turn them into little daily or weekly rituals, filling your life with sunshine.

Quite simply, enjoy simple pleasures and rituals – and you will be happy.

Rule #15 –
Accept What Is

"Happiness is a function of accepting what is."
– Werner Erhard

How many of us *fight* against what is happening in our lives?

In our family? In society? In the world around us?

You get fined for parking illegally. We've all done it at some point or another. You've checked it out, you were wrong, and there's little you can do about it.

Do you just shrug it off, accept what is, and continue happily with your day?

Or, more realistically, do you moan about it for the next three days – sharing your woes with everyone you meet? Do you let it put you in a bad mood? Anger you? Taint your day?

If you're like most people, you do the latter.

And that's just a simple example.

You might be fighting against your teenage son's quest for freedom. Or society's uncomfortable take on your sexuality. Or the way you look.

Or, quite simply, you might generally be fighting against the cards life has dealt you.

I'm not saying that you shouldn't take action to *change* the world around you. With discussion, or protests, or dieting.

But does all of that pent-up anger and resentment really *serve* anything?

Rather than fighting it *internally*, wouldn't it be much better just to accept what is *first* – and then change what you want, if you still want to?

The world is a rough place. Sometimes things can get pretty crappy. Make no mistake: when it rains, it pours. And the people that live here? A lot of them are pretty foolish. So, I'm on your side here. You're *right*.

But it's pointless holding onto emotions that are holding you back.

By not *accepting* (or *welcoming*, or *embracing*, or whatever other word you may prefer) what is, you are pushing against what exists right now. That causes tension, which results in stress, limitation, and a lack of clarity.

By *accepting*, welcoming, embracing what is, you clear all of your emotions. Your thoughts gain more clarity. You become happier. You experience more freedom.

If you *can* change things, after accepting them, you'll have a sharper mind and more energy to do so. If you can't change things, or if you're trying to change other people, stop immediately – realise that you simply can't, and move onto something else.

Pointless worrying – there's nothing you can do about it. Shrug and smile about it, that's life.

Just accept what is – and you will be happy.

Rule #16 –
Exercise and
Eat Well

*"If more of us valued food and
cheer and song above hoarded
gold, it would be a merrier
world." – J.R.R.Tolkien*

This book is crammed with rules for helping you
achieve happiness.

Some rules are philosophies, providing you with
fresh ways of experiencing the world. Others are
techniques, enabling you to deal with the world in
a more positive manner.

**But others – like this one – are really darn
practical!**

You see, research shows that both exercise and "feel good food" can have a DRAMATIC effect on your happiness levels!

Firstly, moderate exercise at least three times a week can rocket your serotonin, phenyl ethylamine and endorphin levels. These are the natural "feel good" chemicals that put a smile on your face.

Here's something else: The best kind of exercise you can get to feel happy doesn't even require a gym membership!

Just walk for around forty minutes a day to enjoy the best happiness boost possible. You'll not only benefit from serotonin, melatonin and adrenaline increases, you'll also boost oxygen levels in your brain, thereby increasing focus and short-term memory. Not to mention that after a short while, you'll begin enjoying a trimmer body, helping to heighten your self-esteem.

Secondly, eating the right kind of foods can make you a much happier person.

For example, did you know that your Omega 3 (fatty fish oil) levels can seriously affect how happy you are? In Germany, where fish consumption is low owing to geography, depression levels are high. Yet in Japan, with sushi-bars on every street corner, depression is a much rarer condition.

So what are the perfect foods to eat for making you happier?

Well, almost ALL types of fish and nut work wonders. You can also try turkey, asparagus, sunflower seeds, cottage cheese, pineapple, tofu spinach, bananas and lobster.

These foods are high in tryptophan, an amino acid the body converts into serotonin, bringing about greater states of wellbeing. (For a full breakdown of feel good foods, read Appendix 4.)

For actual full meals *designed* to boost your happiness, try visiting the Food and Mood project, online at www.foodandmood.org – and checking out their Mind Meal options.

And don't forget your daily vitamin and mineral supplements, too – especially Omega 3. Brain supplements, such as Acuity (www.acuitydirect.com) can also help.

That's how you can change your happiness levels – just by changing what you put into your mouth.

So, make sure that *you* eat well and exercise – and you will be happy.

Rule #17 – Zoom Out and Don't Sweat

"If you do not raise your eyes
you will think that you
are the highest point."
- Antonio Porchia

Right now, you have a set of priorities running in your life.

Number one may be that business deal you're working on. Number two could be the mortgage you're really trying to pay off. Number three is that vacation, and whether you're really going to get on with Aunt Marjorie for two whole weeks.

These are your current priorities.

But isn't it funny how life can sometimes jolt any of us right back down to earth – and remind us all of what *really* matters in life? Of what our *real* priorities should be?

I'm talking about the perspective we gain after a family member passes away. Or after a near-miss motorcycle accident. Or the moment your first child arrives into the world.

We suddenly zoom out and view the world from a million miles above.

Petty arguments are no longer worth our attention. The "importance" of business seems to disappear immediately. All we often want to do is express our love for those we care about.

Life has a habit of reminding us of the important things, whenever we forget.

Have YOU forgotten what is really important in your life?

Are you sacrificing your family time to clear that never-ending pile of paperwork? Do you spend days moaning about the negative, getting angered by the smallest of comments? Did you last hold yourself back from telling your partner how you felt – because you were embarrassed?

Here's the simple truth: You might be dead one hour from now.

You *never, ever* know what is around the corner. So, try regularly "zooming out" of your current picture, and realizing the true priorities in your life. If you can, do it every day - particularly when you return home from work.

Then kick back your shoes, and enjoy some quality time with family and friends.

Life is short.

As GoDaddy.com CEO Bob Parsons says, we're not here for a long time, we're here for a good time.

So, zoom out regularly, don't sweat the small stuff – and you will be happy.

Rule #18 – Laugh, Dance, Smile!

"A friendly look, a kindly smile, one good act, and life's worthwhile." - Unknown

You know, it's funny...

The other week, I decided to attend a local Buddhist class. They were holding a discussion on the nature of happiness. The "enlightened one" entered centre stage, a gentle, snail-paced walk to match his speech, and talked about what made us happy.

This went on for a period of two hours, with many questions from the small audience.

But here's the thing.

The teacher never smiled or laughed once the whole time. Not only that, neither did the

audience! Enlightenment? Doubtful. Boredom?
Definitely.

True happiness, self-development, freedom,
comes from inside - and is expressed externally in
bright faces, a big smile, and plenty of laughing.
Just look at the Dalai Lama.

Once you've applied the rules in this book, you'll
automatically find yourself being a happier,
jollier person – naturally! But why not give it all a
little helping hand?

This rule is a reminder that you should *surround
yourself with happiness* – and just watch it rub off
on you!

How?

Get dancing, for a start! Studies show dancing to
be the absolute BEST way to immediately rocket
your happiness. It boosts serotonin levels,
promotes good health and weight loss, and allows
you to indulge in essential human and body
contact.

But it doesn't stop there. Why not also...

Keep feel-great music CDs in your car. Cover the
walls of your home with uplifting pictures.
Watch more comedy movies. Listen to positive
tunes on your iPod while working. Indulge in *The
Simpsons* or *Family Guy*, and laugh at life itself.

Heck, when it comes to that, give yourself a pat on the back for being the big, crazy screw-up that you are!

Laugh at all of the silly problems you've been holding on to, so very well, for so long. Laugh that you're even mad enough to read a book like this. Laugh that you're alive, and that so many opportunities are open to you – right now.

That's why I think the Dalai Lama laughs so much.

He's realised the crazy, wonderful, ridiculous nature of life – and that the *real* meaning of us being here, if there is a meaning, is to be happy.

So, right now – laugh, dance, smile – and you will be happy.

The 18 Rules of Happiness – Review

Rule #1 - Stop Feeling Sorry for Yourself!

Self-pity is the very worst kind of emotion. It destroys everything around itself, and leaves you feeling powerless. Stop being the victim, stop feeling sorry for yourself – and be happy.

Rule #2 – Be Grateful

The world is so fast-paced that we're rarely grateful of its gifts. Think of all the things you're grateful for right now: family, health, home, everything. Spend time being grateful each day – and be happy.

Rule #3 – Say Yes More

We each say "No!" way too often. Try saying "Yes!" more to all of life's experiences. Don't fight the river's current. Say "Yes!" more to emotions, situations, social invitations – and be happy.

Rule #4 – Follow Your Bliss

In life, we often find ourselves half-way up a
ladder we don't want to climb, rather than at the
bottom of one we do. What do you really want to
be? Follow your own bliss – and be happy.

Rule #5 – Learn to Let Go

Emotions often hold us back from true happiness
and freedom. Remember, you are not your
emotions. Let go of unwanted emotions by asking
yourself "Can I let this go?" Do it – and be happy.

Rule #6 – Do Random Acts of Kindness

Being kind is double-edged. It makes you feel
happier, and spreads that joy to someone else too.
Do more Random Acts of Kindness every day –
smile, hold open a door, pay for a coffee – and be
happy.

Rule #7 – Happiness Is Only Ever Now

Most of us spend our time anywhere but in the
present. We obsess about the past, or plan for the
future. Now is the only time that really exists.
Make the decision to be happy – now.

Rule #8 – Experience, Don't Hoard!

Research shows that material purchases only
boost your happiness levels temporarily.
Experiences bring more overall joy. Enjoy safari

holidays, learn a language, join a dancing group –
and be happy.

Rule #9 – Appreciate Both Sides of the Coin

How many times do we try to embrace happiness
– and reject sadness? They're both sides of the
same coin. You cannot have one without the other.
Sadness is critical. Don't fight it – and be happy.

Rule #10 – Be More Social

Extensive research shows that the happiest and
most successful people are those with large social
networks. How many friends do you have? Be
proactive, start making more – and become
happier.

Rule #11 – Love More!

The more you love, the happier you are. Try
giving everyone and everything around you a
little more love. Friends, family, nature, even
enemies – open your heart, give them love – and
be happy.

Rule #12 – Have a Dream

Dreams are the spark plugs of the spirit. They give
each day excitement and enable you to move
forward. What are your dreams? Think about it,
write them down. Then do them – and be happy.

Rule #13 – Intention Sets Direction

The outcome you expect is usually the one you receive. If you don't know where you're going, any road will take you there. So, set a great intention in everything you do – and be happy.

Rule #14 – Enjoy Simple Pleasures

Real happiness can be found in simple pleasures and rituals. From a daily walk in nearby countryside to a glass of wine after work. Indulge in these, setup your own little rituals – and be happy.

Rule #15 – Accept What Is

Many of us spend time resisting what is. We fight against our own emotions, building up anger and resentment. Accept what is right now. Change it if you can. But accept it first – and be happy.

Rule #16 – Exercise and Eat Well

You are as happy as your lifestyle! For optimum happiness, try walking for 40 minutes a day. Take Omega 3 supplements, and eat more fish, nuts, turkey, cottage cheese. Enjoy – and be happy.

Rule #17 – Zoom Out and Don't Sweat

We often get a fresh perspective on life, after we
lose a family member, or survive an illness. Don't
wait for life to remind you. Zoom out and
remember your real priorities now – and be
happy.

Rule #18 – Laugh, Dance, Smile!

Take time to laugh at the craziness of life! Splash
out and enjoy to the max. Surround yourself with
happiness – wonderful music, dance classes,
evenings with friends. Smile – and be happy!

Conclusion

"If you want to be happy, be." - Leo Tolstoy

Happiness is easier than we think.

As you might have realised, it's not really about what's happening out there in the world. But rather what's happening here – inside ourselves.

Every single one of us has the capacity for infinite happiness, if only we open ourselves to it.

Remember, the sun is *always* shining brightly.

It never stops.

It's just that most people look to the sky and end up seeing the grey clouds that cover it. They focus on that gloom and doom. They're immersed in negativity.

Using the "rules" in this book, you've discovered a handful of powerful methods for clearing those grey clouds – so you can realise the bright, shiny happiness hiding just behind.

Embrace these techniques. Practice them daily. Re-read this book at least a dozen times. Let these philosophies become a part of your everyday existence. It'll pay off more than you can imagine.

You'll become smarter, more content, more successful – and, of course, happier.

So, give me a great big SMILE right now – and know that I'm smiling right back at you!

Thank you for reading,

Karl Moore
www.karlmoore.com

Appendices

Appendix 1 – A Short Course in Releasing

Releasing is a fantastic tool for unleashing freedom in your life!

It allows you to let go of sadness and limitation, and embrace freedom and happiness. It enables you to drop negative emotion and increase positive emotion.

Releasing allows you to control your feelings, rather than letting your feelings control you.

In fact, I'd consider releasing to be perhaps the most important self-development technique on the planet.

Sound interesting? Well, let's start from the beginning.

Emotions are how we *feel*.

We feel *grief* after the death of a family member. We feel *anger* when somebody rubs us up the wrong way. We feel *pride* when we do a great job.

Emotions are useful, and help make us human.

But sometimes emotions hold us back.

They cause us to freeze in *fear* when about to deliver our speech. They cause us to continue being *angry* toward someone we should've forgiven long ago. They cause us to carry on being *addicted* to gambling, or bad relationships.

Yes, emotions have a lot to answer for!

But the good thing is that you can control your emotions just as simply as you'd control a light switch. Turning them off is as simple as *<click>*.

You see, the secret you must realise is this:

You are not your emotions.

That's right. You are not your emotions. And your emotions are not you.

Emotions are just things that you *experience*.

Rather than "I am angry," a more accurate description might be "I am experiencing anger."

And rather than "I am courageous," a more lucid version may be "I am feeling courageous."

So, emotions are just things you experience. Sometimes they feel good, sometimes they run riot. And you can switch them off as easily as you'd switch off a plug socket.

How?

Through the process of *releasing*.

Now, releasing is all about letting go of your negative emotions. When you let go of negative emotions, you'll feel lighter and more stress-free. You'll enjoy greater freedom and feel more at peace with the world.

Releasing is always a great idea.

(You can let go of positive emotions too, and you'll typically feel even more positive as a result.)

How can you release?

Firstly, you need to recognize that we're each desperately holding onto our emotions – even those emotions that aren't serving us. We're clenching them, like we'd clench our hands around a pencil or a small ball.

We're holding on to that *fear*, that *grief*, that *apathy* – because we somehow think that it is *us*, and that we *need* it.

But when we realize that we are not our emotions, and that we don't need a particular emotion, we can simply choose to let it go.

That is, we can unclench our fist – and allow that emotion to simply be free, or even drop out of our hands altogether.

Let's try it together.

Think of something right now that you know is a concern for you. It might be a situation at work, or a particular person you dislike, or just some general worry that you have. Make it a simple issue for now, just for starters.

Think of that thing, and notice the resistance that builds up in your stomach.

Then simply ask yourself the question:

"Can I let this go?"

Which is another way of saying: Can you unclench the grip you have around this feeling right now? Can you release the grip? Can you let go of the resistance? Can you just drop the *emotion* attached to this issue?

As you ask yourself "Can I let this go?" – breathe out, and answer honestly with "Yes" or "No" out loud. It doesn't matter which you answer with, it'll all provide you with an emotional release on some level.

While exhaling, *feel* the release happening. Feel yourself unclenching that grip. Feel yourself just letting go of that emotion. Notice the difference?

Remember, *we* are the ones that are holding on to our emotions. We are the ones that are causing them to continue living inside our minds.

Would you prefer to hold on to your negative emotions even more, allowing them to bubble away inside your mind – or would you prefer to just let them go?

Remember, by letting go, we're not agreeing with it, or letting somebody off the hook. We're simply releasing the *emotion* attached to it. We're granting *ourselves* greater peace and serenity.

Then, when you're ready, connect to see whether that issue still has any charge.

If it does, repeat the process once more: connect with the issue, ask yourself "Can I let this go?", answer "Yes" or "No" while breathing out, and *feel* the release.

Loop on this entire process a few more times.

You'll soon begin to really *feel* very different about the whole issue.

Within minutes, you'll notice the emotion has drastically reduced in size – and may just have disappeared altogether. Right?

Finished? How did that feel?

Let's try it once more. This time, make sure you follow through the entire process. Out loud, too, if you can.

Again, think of a situation which brings up some resistance in your tummy. It might be an annoying person, or a small worry that you have right now.

Get in touch with that sensation, that energy, that feeling. Then ask yourself:

"Can I let this go?"

Answer the question out loud, with a "Yes" or "No," while breathing out. Remember, any answer is fine, they both work the same magic. Just be honest.

As you answer, loosen your clutch on the emotion. Relax into the comfort. *Release*.

Feel yourself unclenching. Feel yourself *letting go*.

Releasing feels great. It's like the feeling you get when the doctors call you, after those worrying tests – and say you've got the all clear. It's total relief. That's releasing.

To help you feel the release even further, imagine two doors in front of your stomach opening, allowing all of the negative emotion just to flow out – as you let go. Really *feel* it happening. Great!

Finished?

Now check how you feel.

If there's still any emotional charge left, no worries. That's fine! Repeat the process until you feel better about the issue, or want to finish.

If you don't feel any progress at all, don't worry either. Just let go of trying to get results.

Sometimes you're too busy "watching" to really experience.

And if you answer "No" during the process and don't feel yourself able to let go, don't worry about that either. Every step, no matter how redundant it may feel, helps take you closer to emotional freedom. Just release on it and move on.

And that's it, really.

Releasing is the quickest and easiest method for letting go of troublesome emotions.

It's the hidden process behind almost every therapy out there – from psychotherapy to tribal drum therapy. Except here we're just releasing the emotions directly, rather than fluffing up the process.

There's no need to spend years sitting on a couch, going into your "back story" and analyzing precisely *why* things happened that way. Here, we just release – and move on.

It really is as simple as that.

Just connect with the emotion and ask yourself: "Can I let this go?" – then breathe out, answer "Yes" or "No," and *feel* yourself letting go.

Easy!

Further Releasing Methods

There are other ways of releasing, too – all based on the same core "letting go" principle.

One of the most popular is the *three questions* method.

This was popularized by the late Lester Levenson, and is now taught in the Abundance Course (www.releasetechnique.com) and The Sedona Method (www.sedona.com).

This technique is based on the following premises:

1. We *don't know* that we can let emotions go
2. We *don't want* to let go of emotions
3. We always *put off* letting go until later

So, this method of releasing works by addressing each of these questions – allowing us to cycle through, and slowly let go of the emotions that are holding us back.

Here are the steps:

1. Think of the situation, and connect with the emotion you'd like to release.
2. Ask yourself: "*Could* I let this go?" (yes/no - answer out loud, honestly)
3. Move on to ask: "*Would* I let this go?" (again, yes/no)

4. And then: "*When?*" (now/later)
5. Feel that release – then check to see how the situation feels. If there's still some emotional charge, go back to step one and loop again: you'll find some issues are layered like onions, and are released over multiple passes. Or if you feel stuck in the actual process itself, let go of "wanting to feel stuck," and start again – or rest for a while.

Another popular releasing method is the *welcoming* technique, popularized by many releasing teachers, including Chris Payne with his Effort-Free Life System (www.effortfree.com).

Here are the steps to follow for this technique:

1. Lower your head and place your hand on your chest or stomach. Get in touch with an emotion, or a situation that has an emotional charge for you.
2. Notice the intensity of the feeling in your body, and rate the intensity from 0 to 10.
3. *Welcome* the emotion, much as you'd welcome a friend into your home. Welcoming doesn't mean you agree or forgive the emotion, just embrace it, accept it, *welcome* it. Allow it to be there, instead of pretending it doesn't exist. Feel the welcoming.

4. Now get in touch with the emotion again. How does it feel?
5. Rate the intensity again, from 0 to 10. Keep going until it comes down to 0. If you feel stuck, ask yourself if you could let go of trying to change being stuck – or simply continue later.

Releasing teacher Lester Levenson (whose work is now continued through The Abundance Course and The Sedona Method) also used to suggest that individuals try letting go of wanting *control, approval* and *security* too. These are general terms that can help you release on emotions right across the board.

You know, releasing is all about letting go of emotions. It's about detachment.

It's what the Eastern world calls letting go of our *attachments* and *aversions*.

In the Western world, this releasing process is essentially the equivalent of saying:

"F**k it!"

(A wonderful argument set forth by John C. Parkin in his book of the same name.)

Try each of these techniques yourself, and start using whichever suits you best. But remember to *try* them.

Releasing isn't just for reading about. It's *experiential*.

Conclusion

Releasing is a powerful method for gaining greater emotional freedom.

It helps you realize that you are not your emotions – and thereby allows you to release all of the limiting thoughts, emotions and feelings that have held you back in the past.

You'll become happier, enjoy more self-empowerment, and simply be more free when you discover releasing for yourself.

Take time out to go through all of your issues, negative emotions, and the people in your life – releasing on each in turn. You'll feel the benefits immediately.

Just keep asking yourself "Can I let this go?"

Practice it as often as you can – and do it all the time. Even when you're talking to somebody, you can release there and then, in that moment. It's simple and it's easy.

To learn more about releasing, I'd suggest one of the following books:

• The Sedona Method – by Hale Dwoskin – www.sedona.com

- The Abundance Course – by Larry Crane - www.releasetechnique.com
- The Secret of Letting Go – by Guy Finley – www.guyfinley.com
- Effort-Free Life System – by Chris Payne – www.effortfree.com
- F**k It – by John C. Parkin – www.thefuckitway.com

Discover releasing for yourself, embrace it in your daily life – and I promise you'll never look back.

Even if that releasing is as simple as saying "F**k it!" just a little more often.

Appendix 2 – Inspiring Quotes to Make You Smile

Life has a habit of throwing crazy situations our way, giving us chance to demonstrate our character in the way we handle them.

But one thing's for sure, we're never the first person in that situation. The whole plethora of human emotion has been experienced googol times by a billion other people.

And that's why quotes are great.

They help us to connect with other people's wisdom, and to learn from our cumulative experiences of life.

That's why this section contains some of my favourite ever quotes – to help inspire you during the times you need it.

A ship is safe in harbor... But that's not what ships were built for - *William Shed*

There is nothing either good or bad... But thinking makes it so - *William Shakespeare*

All that we are is the result of what we have thought. The mind is everything. What we think, we become - *Buddha*

The cave you most fear to enter contains the greatest treasure – *Joseph Campbell*

Life is not measured by its length, but by its depth - *Anonymous*

If you can imagine it, you can achieve it. If you can dream it, you can become it - *William A. Ward*

Life is without meaning. You bring the meaning to it. The meaning of life is whatever you ascribe it to be. Being alive is the meaning – *Joseph Campbell*

There is one quality which one must possess to win, and that is definiteness of purpose, the knowledge of what one wants, and a burning desire to possess it - *Napoleon Hill*

The people who get on in this world are the people who get up and look for the circumstances they want and if they can't find them, make them - *George Bernard Shaw*

The pessimist sees difficulty in every opportunity. The optimist sees the opportunity in every difficulty - *Winston Churchill*

Put yourself in a state of mind where you say to yourself, 'Here is an opportunity for me to celebrate like never before, my own power, my own ability to get myself to do whatever is necessary' - *Martin Luther King, Jr.*

We are what we think. All that we are arises with our thoughts. With our thoughts, we make the world - *Buddha*

I try to learn from the past, but I plan for the future by focusing exclusively on the present. That's were the fun is - *Donald Trump*

I can't change the direction of the wind, but I can adjust my sails to always reach my destination - *Jimmy Dean*

I want to sing like the birds sing, not worrying about who hears or what they think - *Rumi*

The highest reward for a person's toil is not what they get for it, but what they become by it - *John Ruskin*

Men are born to succeed, not to fail - *Henry David Thoreau*

I figured that if I said it enough, I would convince the world that I really was the greatest - *Muhammad Ali*

Happiness is not having what you want. It is wanting what you have - *Unknown*

Success is getting what you want. Happiness is wanting what you get - *Dale Carnegie*

The talent for being happy is appreciating and liking what you have, instead of what you don't have - *Woody Allen*

When you come to a fork in the road, take it - *Yogi Berra*

Fortune favours the bold - *Virgil*

He who lives in harmony with himself lives in harmony with the universe - *Marcus Aurelius*

If you haven't got charity in your heart, you have the worst kind of heart trouble - *Bob Hope*

It is not length of life, but depth of life - *Ralph Waldo Emerson*

Everything that happens happens as it should, and if you observe carefully, you will find this to be so - *Marcus Aurelius*

Act as if it were impossible to fail - *Dorothea Brande*

If you do not conquer self, you will be conquered by self - *Napoleon Hill*

Nobody can go back and start a new beginning, but anyone can start today and make a new ending. - *Maria Robinson*

The future depends on what we do in the present - *Mahatma Gandhi*

Dream as if you'll live forever, live as if you'll die today - *James Dean*

Attain to the place where no one and no thing can disturb you - *Lester Levenson*

When one door of happiness closes, another opens, but often we look so long at the closed door that we do not see the one that has been opened for us - *Helen Keller*

In the hopes of reaching the moon men fail to see the flowers that blossom at their feet - *Albert Schweitzer*

All the world's a stage, And the men and women merely players. They have their exits and their entrances; And one man in his time plays many parts - *William Shakespeare*

If you do not change direction, you may end up where you're heading - *Lao Tzu*

History will be kind to me for I intend to write it - *Winston Churchill*

Appendix 3 – Happy Songs for Your Collection!

Most of us forget just how much music affects our mood!

So, find out what music makes you happy, and surround yourself with it. Load it onto your iPhone, create a mix CD for your car, play it on your computer at work.

And if you're unsure what makes you happy, here are a few fantastic suggestions to get you started!

Fascination - *Alphabeat*

Wake Up Boo! – *Boo Radleys* (Proven in scientific studies to be the 'happiest song in the world!')

She Moves in Her Own Way – *The Kooks*

Love Train – *The O'Jays*

The Voice of Truth – *Casting Crowns*

Shiny Happy People – *REM*

I'm Working My Way Back to You Babe – *The Spinners*

Sunshine, Lollipops & Rainbows – *Lesley Gore*

Search For The Hero - *Heather Small: M People*

Don't Worry Be Happy – *Jimmy Cliff* or *Bobby McFerrin*

What A Wonderful World – *Louis Armstrong*

We Are The Champions – *Queen*

Simply The Best – *Tina Turner*

If You Want to Sing Out – *Cat Stevens*

I Had The Time Of My Life - *Bill Medley & Jennifer Warne*

My Way - *Frank Sinatra*

Greatest Love Of All – *Whitney Houston*

You've Got A Friend – *Carole King*

All You Need Is Love - *The Beatles*

Ray Of Light - *Madonna*

Headstart For Happiness - *The Style Council*

I Can See Clearly Now - *Jimmy Cliff, Johnny Nash* or *Bob Marley*

We Will Rock You – *Queen*

Wind Beneath My Wings – *Bette Midler* or *Colleen Hewitt*

O Happy Day - *Sister Act*

Paint The Sky With Stars – *Enya*

Orinoco Flow - *Enya*

Good Morning Starshine - *Serena Ryder*

Walking On Sunshine - *Katrina and The Waves*

I Believe I Can Fly - *R. Kelly*

Chariots Of Fire - *Vangelis*

Return To Innocence - *Enigma*

I Feel Good - *James Brown*

Beautiful Day - *U2*

New Day - *Celine Dion*

Eye Of The Tiger - *Survivor*

O Fortuna - *Carmina Burana by Carl Orff*

Nessun Dorma - *from Puccini's opera Turandot*

Lovely Day - *Bill Withers*

The Roses Of Success - *Chitty Chitty Bang Bang soundtrack*

Rocky Theme Tune

Appendix 4 – Feel Good Foods

A nutritious, balanced diet is the key to good health and longevity. But did you know that some foods actually enhance mood and help maintain those all-important feel-good vibes?

Eating for happiness - as well as health - should be your primary goal. To obtain the sustenance you need, include the following foods in your diet:

- **Foods high in Omega 3 – ie, oily fish, nuts, flax seeds.** Omega 3 has been scientifically proven to reduce depression and increase happiness. Try also taking a daily supplement, too

- **Foods rich in tryptophan – ie, lobster, turkey, pineapple, tofu, bananas.** Tryptophan is converted by the body into the feel-good chemical serotonin, which increases your well-being

- **Foods with plenty of amino-acids – ie, chicken, turkey, fish, cheese, cottage cheese,** eggs, milk, nuts, pulses, bananas, avocados, wheat germ, and legumes. These foods help maintain correct amino acid levels, essential in balancing your mood

- **Foods which raise vitamin B levels – ie, spinach, peas, orange juice, wheat germ or avocado**. Solid vitamin B levels help safeguard yourself against depression

Also:

- **Whole grains such as oats, quinoa or brown rice** contain B vitamins to ensure the slow release of sugars needed to maintain well-being

- **Carbohydrates, such as cereals, rice, pasta and starchy vegetables** provide slow energy release to maintain a balanced metabolism

- **Regular 'energy snacks' such as fruit, cereal, seeds and nuts** help maintain energy levels and good mood throughout the day

- **Pomegranates, goji berries, blueberries, raspberries, avocados, mangoes, apples, macadamia nuts, spirulina, broccoli and spinach** – all super-foods that contribute to overall wellness

And remember these feel-good food pointers:

- Vitamins and minerals – especially the B vitamins – are essential for correct functioning of the nervous system and help to prevent illness linked to depression, anxiety or dementia. Vitamin D supplements have been shown to help with Seasonal Affective Disorder (SAD). Always take a good multi-vitamin and mineral supplement

- Ditch adrenalin-fuelling coffee and choose relaxing herbal and fruit teas to aid tranquillity and boost well-being. Also drink a few glasses of water each day to maintain correct hydration

- Eat fresh, organic foods where possible. Choose raw veggie or fruit options

- Replace junk foods (high sugar / high salt / high fat / high additives content) with natural foods – vegetables, fruit, grains and seeds

- Always eat in moderation

- Believe in the healing properties of the food you're eating

- Enjoy your food! Hang up your worries and frustrations before you sit down for dinner. When you think calm and happy thoughts while you're eating, it will aid your digestion and ensure that the food provides you with the energy and healing needed

Treat your body well. It's the only one you have.

Good nutrition is essential to maintain optimum state of mind, body and spirit. What you choose to eat makes a real difference, so choose the perfect ingredients for a happy you!

For more information on how food can affect your mood, alongside ideal meal plans for your mind, visit www.foodandmood.org.

Appendix 5 –
Claim Your FREE
MP3 Version of
This Book!

Do you learn better by listening, rather than reading?

Don't have time to read the full 18 rules right now?

No problem. We've created an MP3 version of this entire book for you to download – so that you can listen whenever you get a spare few minutes.

On your computer, on your iPod, or in your car!

To download your copy, simply visit www.the18rules.com.

You may be required to answer a security question before being given the download link.

You can also buy the official audio version of this book – "The 18 Rules of Happiness" – in the iTunes store.

Enjoy!

Made in the USA
Monee, IL
05 November 2020